CW00566230

Good Company II

Good Company II

A further Anthology of
sayings, stories and
answers to questions by
His Holiness
Shantanand Saraswati
1961—1993

THE STUDY SOCIETY

LONDON

ISBN 978-0-9547939-9-9
A catalogue record for this book is available from the British Library

Published in 2009 by The Society for the Study of Normal Psychology,
Colet House, 151 Talgarth Road, London W14 9DA
Telephone: 0208 748 9338, Fax: 0208 563 0551,
Email: colethouse@clara.net,
Website: http://www.studysociety.net

Printed in Great Britain by the
MPG Books Group,
Bodmin and King's Lynn

Contents

*"The spiritual world is concerned with only one subject:
freedom and appreciation of unchanging truth."*

Introduction

During the early years of the last century the great Russian philosopher, writer and mathematician P.D.Ouspensky became convinced that there must exist an ancient system of thought lying at the root of the various religious and philosophical systems that have arisen in recent millennia. Until the outbreak of the First World War he travelled extensively looking for traces of this system, especially in India, but could not find it. Owing to the Revolution in Russia he travelled via the Middle East to Western Europe and eventually settled in London, where he began to share his ideas with a circle of like-minded people.

Among them was Dr Francis Roles, a practising physician and man of remarkable culture and spiritual sensitivity, who admitted that Mr Ouspensky was, "The first man I could really trust." Their work centred on the observation that ordinarily we forget who we are, because in the process of observing ourselves we never remember ourselves—our consciousness and attention are constantly changing. Various methods were tried in the attempt to 'Self-remember' but it remained apparent that some vital knowledge was missing.

The onset of the Second World War disrupted their work, but before Mr Ouspensky died in 1947 he asked Dr Roles to continue the search for the ancient Tradition which he felt would reveal not only the source of special Knowledge but also a simple method which could enable people to realise their full potential.

It was in 1961 that Dr Roles, while in India, met a master of the ancient Advaita (non-dualism) Tradition, the Shankara-charya of Jyotir Math of Northern India, His Holiness Shantanand Saraswati. He immediately recognised that here was a man who embodied 'Self-remembering' and the ancient Tradition he was looking for. The respect each man felt for the other was immediate and mutual. Here at last was a man who could answer, in a most convincing way, all the questions put to him. Mr Ouspensky's wish had been fulfilled.

Meetings took place between them, mainly in Allahabad, until the death of Dr Roles in 1982, and continued with his colleagues until 1993. A Record of all the dialogues, stories, questions and answers which took place during these meetings was made by The Study Society, extracts from which are now being made more widely available.

Here is a second collection of extracts. The first collection was published as *Good Company** in 1987 and contained quotations taken from audiences up until 1985. This further selection includes answers taken from the Record of later meetings.

It is hoped that in presenting this further volume, a significant contribution will be made to the deepening perception across the planet that we are all united as human beings by a common heritage of eternal wisdom, which does not change over the millennia. But to realise it fully His Holiness stresses the need to combine our knowledge of this wisdom with a deepening of our own Being, or con-sciousness, so that it becomes practical. The method he advocates for bringing this about is the regular and sincere practice of meditation.

Several Sanskrit words appear in the replies to questions, some of which have no exact English equivalent. While translating from Hindi and Sanskrit into the English language is not always easy, His Holiness nonetheless encouraged us to do so. His wish was for us to express the ideas in plain English so that everyone could comprehend their meaning.

Dr Roles was well aware of this challenge. Back in 1972, in the Foreword to his book, *A Lasting Freedom**, he wrote:

"Modern languages (which have grown up in a haphazard way on the basis of practical communication) are deficient in words to describe psychological and spiritual experience. In contrast, some ancient languages, like Sanskrit, having been consciously framed to express the inner world as well as the outer world, have many additional words which bring out the finer shades of meaning.

"In addition, (English) words are continually being devalued by their popular use, and to be understood they must be redefined in accordance with spiritual experience."

Here then is a brief glossary of both Sanskrit and English terms used in the text which may help you to understand their meaning more fully. (It is not intended for the Sanskrit scholar.) Some words can have several meanings depending on the context in which they are used, and some have no clear definition. But even more important than meaning is the experience we gain from them as our souls become ever more enriched.

☆

---

*Obtainable from the Study Society.

Glossary

Advaita
Non-dual—without a second. School of Vedantic thought associated with the name of Shankara, based on the truth that there is nothing separate from or other than the divine. The Absolute is one: no particle or aspect of anything (concerning body or mind) can have a separate existence by itself.

Aham and Ahamkar
Aham refers to universal I or ego which is unconditional. **Ahamkar** refers to ego as experienced by an individual—kar meaning vehicle—in which the pure Self (Atman) is reflected. Described as 'pure' or 'impure'. 'Pure' when unconditional or unattached to anything, at one with universal: 'impure' when it becomes the "I-maker" attaching itself to possessions of all kind—me and mine—egoism. One of the four components of soul (antahkaran).

Ananda
The principle of pure Love, happiness or bliss. One of the three attributes of the Absolute. (See also Sat and Chit.)

Antahkaran
All that relates to our psyche or mind, as distinct from our physical body. Sometimes called soul or 'inner instrument', as distinct from the 'outer instrument' of the physical body. All that makes our inner world of experience possible. Has four parts: the thinking mind (manas), the evaluating mind (buddhi), the ego-maker

(ahamkar), and the memory store of all previous experience (chitta).

Atman and Param-atman
Atman is usually translated as Self, the embodiment of universal Self or Being which is called *Param-atman,* the Absolute or Supreme Self: Brahman. It shares the same characteristics of full Consciousness, all Knowledge and innate joy, Love or bliss. The ever-present basis of the consciousness of "I": unmoving, unchanging and eternal, with no gender and favouring everyone impartially. The word 'God' is the nearest equivalent for us.

Buddhi
That aspect of our minds which appreciates qualities and makes decisions/choices: it evaluates and discriminates.

Chit
Universal Consciousness, True Knowledge or Intelligence that exists whether or not we experience it. One of the three attributes of the Absolute (the other two being Sat and Ananda).

Chitta
All that we hold in memory and which can be recalled. Acts like a filing system. (That which can reflect Universal Consciousness, or Chit.)

Dharma
Natural Law. Recognition that the natural world of physical phenomena, human action and thought, are governed by universal law. All things and events are part of an

indivisible whole. Sanatan Dharma (eternal 'religion') is behaviour that is in harmony with this unity. (See under 'Origin of religions').

Gunas
Refer to the three fundamental qualities inherent in everything and every situation. There is no equivalent translation in the English language. *Sattva* is the quality of harmony, balance, goodness, truth, love, happiness: *Rajas* is the quality of movement and activity of any kind: and *Tamas* is the quality of inertia, sleepiness, depression, ignorance. All are present everywhere in varying amounts.

Manas
Is concerned with gathering all information and presenting it, like files, to memory (chitta). For much of the time it is preoccupied with circling thoughts and images.

Samskar (or Sanskar)
Tendencies, traits or habits, some of which we are born with and some we acquire in this life. They give rise to our mental and moral character. They can vary in quality and be modified.

Sat
Existence, reality, that which is always there, Truth, Knowledge. One of the three characteristics of the Absolute (the others being Chit and Ananda.)

Certain English words are also given distinctive meanings.

True Knowledge and knowledge
True Knowledge refers to knowledge of the unseen or inner world which relates to our experience. It is unrelated to time or space and so is true for all time and in all places. All other knowledge relates to the seen or outer, physical world, which is relative to time and space, and so impermanent (changeable). At times referred to the 'Real' and 'unreal' world.

Consciousness
When used with a capital C it refers to universal Consciousness or Chit. Otherwise it refers to the fluctuating individual consciousness of which we are all aware. Much was said in earlier years about 'levels of consciousness' but towards the end of his life Dr. Roles strongly affirmed that "There is only one consciousness. All 'levels' are levels of impediment."

Self
A clear distinction between 'self' and 'Self'. With a small 's' it refers to an individual's consciousness of his own personal identity with its bodily make-up and personal characteristics: assumed to be 'separate' and distinct from all others. When spelt as 'Self' it refers to our true being as one with Universal Being, with all its attributes. Synonymous with Atman—"of one being with the Father." 'Self-remembering' means what it says—the practise of mindfulness.

☆

1 Purpose of life

Q. Ordinarily we think we are separate. Each person has a different life: a different way of expressing themselves. What is the importance of each person finding their own way?

H.H. The purpose of Man is to realise the supreme Truth that the one light of Atman, or ultimate Reality, is in everybody and every particle in creation. Different bodies have different goals but Atman is everywhere the same, and everyone's ultimate goal is to realise Atman. It cannot be seen, but after a life of restraint, if you have the capacity to control your mind, your intellect, your body, then you will see this light. You will realise it and you will become One with it.

The System of Knowledge and method of Meditation are simply to lead people to discriminate between the transitory and the eternal, between that which has form and that which does not, between words and the spirit, so that one can enjoy forms, words and also the real Being.

The purpose of life according to the Eternal way is to be whole, complete and One.

Our true home

Q. Can the various individual spiritual practices be seen as food for Atman? They must all come from the desire of the Absolute. Is everything we do towards realisation for His enjoyment?

H.H. God himself becomes many bodies and His bliss, ananda or joy, is in everybody because He has become everybody. God is the ocean of bliss and from that everybody, every particle, is in God himself. We feel separate but once personal ego is abolished then we realise that we are one with God.

Meditation is more of a coming home, which is very easy. If one meditates faithfully, sincerely, and keeps up continuous efforts, one would be able to comprehend and complete the journey to the real Self very much sooner.

Meditation is a journey back home. Most of the troubles and tribulations which one experiences are in the first part of the journey. When that point is passed you are nearer home. Then there is only one point to look for, and you don't have to bother about anything else. Meditation is going back home—home to the Self.

The kingdom within

Q. During meditation I am sometimes attracted to thoughts and memories which are difficult to turn away from. At other times I find some centre in myself which has no words and from which a light radiates. Is this the state I should be seeking?

H.H. These memories and thoughts which creep into the mind at the time of meditation should not be forced out—one should not try. Let them go. Turn inward to the centre you have described which has no name and form—like a light. So it is, but one should not try to analyse this world which is within. We should just *be there* and come out and use that power and wealth in any worldly activity which is useful and efficient. We never have to work out what is there at the centre: just have the experience and use its power.

Q. My mind cannot conceive that only a small effort is required for such an overwhelming result. Realising the size of what is at stake, I ask, "How can I deserve any of this?" My hand cannot turn the key but remains paralysed.

H.H. What this person calls, "overwhelming result" is not a result—it is naturally there. It is only a question of knowing how to get it and whether you remember to take it. For example, supposing a man's father had told him that there was great wealth buried under the house but the young man had forgotten the spot. If someone reminds him, or he remembers, then he can become rich without working further for it. "Hard work" no doubt will produce something but not the real thing that men need. You simply have to retire, just tune in to it, to get the most of it. All you have to do is to remember to take yourself towards what is natural—the wealth of the Kingdom within you. Everyone deserves this Kingdom, this inner world. If someone's hand becomes paralysed so that the key cannot be turned, they should ask the help of their teacher who could relieve the tension.

Happiness

From the beginning of creation all are after the happiness which is man's nature. But when mankind becomes 'attached' to the objects of happiness, it becomes unnatural and leads to our miseries, distractions, our sorrow and everything we do not want. God in His Majesty, although creating everything, never attaches Himself to anything. He remains impartial. It is His desire that everyone should do their duty but should also remain unattached, with no wish to possess anything in creation.

☆

Ignorance is the root of all suffering by common man. A Teacher knows that the remedy for all ailments is true Knowledge. Everyone is running after more happiness, whether it be in the material or spiritual world. Happiness in the material world is only temporary whereas in the spiritual world it is lasting and permanent. Ailments may be different but both the need and the remedy are the same: true Knowledge. If you are assigned to look after the needs of aspirants, cut the roots of ignorance first.

All religions have as their aim the achievement of happiness or bliss. The differences in religions are not to be found in their aim but in their rituals. These rituals have different forms and characters according to the place and time of their origin. Behind these rituals one can see that the spiritual activities of man are practically the same everywhere.

Ananda is the happiness that comes from practice of Knowledge.

2 Unity in diversity

The true search is to find the unity in diversity.

☆

Take the loss of the sense of duality by considering the example of a real elephant and an artificial one made of felt. They may look alike, but with the real one we look out for our safety, as we might do with the artificial one if we didn't know it was unreal. The coarse material world of the senses is like the artificial elephant: once we know that it is artificial then we know the Real: we establish relations with the Real and don't bother much about the artificial.

☆

The universe is perfect for one who has insight and the vision of total unity, who fears nothing but acts with great compassion whenever misery breaks out. He organises things so as to eradicate misery and provides alternatives to minimise suffering if it happens for some unknown reason.

☆

It is certain that in the state of realisation the individual has been transformed into the universal, and total unity with everything in the universe has taken place without reservation. All sense of separation gets dissolved in that state. Unless such a situation has come to pass, it is essential to continue seeking.

One has to accept that there are divisions, which will remain unless they are resolved. To save one from falling into disunity, one has to accept the concept of co-existence and provide space for communication by which the necessary union can take place. Usually this concept is ignored. If there is a selfish attitude then pretence will abound and no progress can be made. Pretence always employs the language of helping others, mostly on a grand scale, while really one wants to promote oneself by victory over others. The result is divisions in churches, nations, societies and even families.

People should get together and open their hearts and minds to put forward their point of view for action which could lead to unity, without criticising others. In such an atmosphere of tolerance and reason, some convergence is possible. In due course things may change, and trust and respect can be built to achieve unity. Wisdom is available everywhere to be used with love and affection.

The total unity, or real Advaita, takes place when knowledge of the truth is achieved. True knowledge is that the world is an illusion, and there is no difference between the Self and the Absolute. The fullness of this wisdom is at the centre of discrimination, and its thousand petals contain all knowledge. When the soul is purified, then whatever aspect of knowledge is needed is available, like touching the keys of a typewriter to produce the desired letter.

☆

Q. His Holiness once said that Self-realisation was not a gradual process but happened instantaneously, as in the story of the Mahatma and the tamarind tree. What strengthens the devotion and longing for truth sufficiently for such a thing to happen?

H.H. Self-realisation is an instantaneous event. Once it happens it does not disappear. The Self is one and limitless, so nothing really happens to it. It is always the same, ever present, ever conscious and ever blissful. So Self-realisation as an event is almost a misnomer. When one talks about Self-realisation one is really talking about the elimination of hindrances or ignorance, which seem to indicate that one is not realised. Therefore, it is true to say that the elimination of hindrances is a gradual process. Realisation is instantaneous and takes place when ignorance is finally dissolved by way of devotion, reason or action.

☆

The universe is one and perfect within the Absolute, and it is His will that it should remain so. But in illusion and agitation everything seems incomplete, separated and alienated. The fullness, the perfection and the unity held in love is then shattered, and in this ignorance everything looks small. But escape is possible. The way to unity is through meditation, true knowledge, love and devotion.

These ways do not belong to any one individual, group, society or nation for all such concepts are limited and binding. They are in truth universal. Everyone in this universe is looking for love and deserves it, and must get it.

There is no division between any individual and the Param-atman. This message He gives to you and you have to bring it into your life—all divisions must go. By passing on the influence of Param-atman—there is only one influence, that of unity—then we can be of help to others. If we imagine that lacking certain things is the cause of trouble, then possessing them must bring happiness. But you see that it does not.

What brings trouble is ignorance; it is not lack of possessions. And ignorance is of one thing only— ignorance of unity. When we do not know what Param-atman is, or what the Holy Man is saying, we keep on dividing things in our own way and so cause our own troubles.

Once you have acquired some knowledge of unity, you live within yourself. It then makes no difference whether you have money, possessions or position. This is the lesson one has to learn.

Beauty lies in variety and wisdom dwells in unity.

3 Impediments

There is no obstacle which cannot be removed by reason and wisdom. After all, consciousness is not supreme for nothing. Consider vanity and arrogance. Reason can dissolve them only when one sees the obstacle and feels sorry to have stumbled. Obstacles are nothing more than a wrong perception of the goodness provided by the Absolute.

☆

Attachment helps to further a cause one loves, even if it is wrong, while hatred reinforces the rejection and destruction of the cause one hates. Viveka (discrimination between the Real and the unreal) is neutral and transparent. It favours and hinders nothing, but furthers the cause of unity, purity, love, equality and universality associated with the Atman: it leads from individual to universal. To use Buddhi for the individual rather than the universal is the wrong use of Buddhi.

Desires

Q. To sharpen Buddhi (discrimination) and strengthen its resolve to serve the Atman seems very important. Can His Holiness give more guidance?

H.H. The best way to strengthen Buddhi is to refrain from entertaining too many desires. As long as one holds on to hundreds of concepts and ambitions in one's mind,

Buddhi will remain blunt and weak from exhaustion.
Agitation in the mind makes Buddhi ineffectual. How can
law and order prevail when a riot is going on in the mind?
Therefore, one must limit the number of desires. When
problems are few and the mind is not agitated, the light
of Atman can fall on a strong and sharp Buddhi to resolve
them. But it can be used in any direction, for better or
worse. In the light of true knowledge Buddhi works
positively, but if the mind has absorbed attachments and
hatreds then all its functions work negatively.

Q. It has been said that when Buddhi is turned towards
spiritual things then it finds the Self. Apart from
meditation are there other ways we can keep our Buddhi
turned towards the spiritual side?

H.H. Buddhi is next to the Atman. Due to its proximity the
light of Atman, or consciousness, falls first upon it. It is its
nature to work through this light, which is universal. If
Buddhi remains steady and transparent it will work for
the Atman with the full brilliance of the light of
consciousness. But attachments and hatred, which are
divisive, dim that light. They superimpose a cover and
reduce the light. Due to lack of light, resolutions are
always wrong.

When one's child makes a mistake reason demands
discipline, but undue attachment forces one to overlook
the fault of the child one loves. This colours one's
judgement. In a similar way if a person one hates does
brilliantly, one tries to belittle, ignore or abuse them. This

is the usual experience. Reason favours no one because Atman is one, and there is no other to favour or hinder.

Q. How does one know what one deserves, or how one steals from the universe and deprives other people?

H.H. It would be authoritarian for anyone to regulate what others deserve. This question arises at a high level of consciousness when universality is being assimilated in life as a practical proposition. To try to find a measure of what you need to fulfil your role, try cutting out something and see if you can survive naturally with dignity. The problem confronts wise householders. If your economies begin to hinder family life, education or your professional work, then you have reached a limit. Anything extra must be returned to society. The fewer desires you entertain the happier you become. Desires have no limit because the world is full of beautiful things. So why not reduce desires and remain free and, therefore, happy.

☆

As long as one is engaged in life one has to work, but when one has renounced all desire to fulfil one's own needs, and devotes one's life to serving others, then the pattern changes. The universe then begins to provide all that is required.

☆

Variety and diversity in creation is the will of the Absolute for the entertainment of the Self. But during the entertainment, when someone becomes attached to one or other aspect, dislike can turn to hatred. Hate leads to conflict which the Absolute did not create: it is not part of the original design. God has not created a quarrelsome universe but a loving one. Conflict is the outcome of attachments and desires, so one should try to refrain from them. If one is unable to eradicate attachments from the minds of others, at least one should eradicate them from one's own mind. With a strong desire to do so, help can be given with love and affection. Without such a desire then scriptures and wisdom cannot help. Shri Krishna in the Bhagavadgita says:

> *"This knowledge may not be explained to those who lack self-discipline and devotion and have no desire to serve, nor to those who speak ill of Me. He who teaches this supreme secret to My devotees, showing the highest devotion to Me, shall doubtless come to Me."*

Transformation depends upon an overriding desire to transform. Although the Self is perfect, superimpositions seem to abound. One must have some deep desire to look for ways of purifying unhelpful habits. Creation is threefold; some people are predominantly sattvic, others are rajasic or tamasic. Those under the influence of tamas are very rigid. Whatever view they hold they presume it to be the only one. The Absolute provides for everyone, but only true seekers make the effort to enlighten themselves through enquiry, reason, devotion and meditation. When more individuals change, society becomes more unified. Beauty lies in variety and wisdom dwells in unity. Creation is governed by the laws of nature which are the expression of love. Nature assists those who seek transformation and punishes those who are attached to rigidity and do not want to change. This is what one has to learn.

☆

Q. Could H.H. say more about control of strong desires?

H.H. The best way to control desires is to have contentment—the feeling that God alone is the best judge of what is best for me: what He has given is best for me. If you have that kind of contentment then you will be able to control strong desires: you will feel happy in whatever circumstances you are placed. A person who can bear with adversities will always remain happy, in the knowledge that we are all part and parcel of Sat-Chit-Ananda. Being happy is a food for Atman.

☆

Q. I have noticed that an underlying desire to get my work finished consumes a great deal of energy. Such an attitude is common in the West and is one of the chief obstacles to our people experiencing deep meditation. We try to cram a lot in a short period of time through desire. Does attachment to the fulfilment of desire rob a man of the energy gained through meditation, or by connecting with the natural Samadhi between desires?

H.H. When you are determined to finish this kind of work there is a burden which causes great loss of energy. If you do not have that determination, but let the thing be done—let it start and let it finish—then that loss of energy will not occur. Work should be done as a part of duty. No work will ever get finished. In big factories, as the bell rings, work is left where it is and later restarted. There is no determination that, "I will not go home until I finish it."

In life everything has a place and every kind of work should get equal importance. Cramping things into a small space means we are robbing some other work of its due importance. One should give equal importance to all aspects of work, and that can only be achieved by regarding it all as your duty. This will not mean any laxity or lethargy.

Thoughts & restless mind

Mental hindrances can be overcome by meditation. Misunderstanding occurs due to the movement in the mind of conflicting desires. For the spiritual traveller Knowledge is like the sun but it is ignorance which leads him away from it. The traveller should not be rushed. He should be encouraged to put down his burden and relax awhile before being shown the proper way.

If a light is continually moved from one point to another, it makes patterns which prevent you from using it or understanding what it is. If it were still, you could understand it and then use it.

Impure thoughts make the mind opaque. If you put red in a glass of water you see things through it as red. If you then add green it becomes even more difficult to see through it. Add more colours and the water becomes opaque and you can see nothing. The mind is like water. You cannot see the Atman through it unless it is clear. Meditation clears it.

Ego

Q. Does 'false I' fall away naturally as one tries to ascend the Ladder, or does it have to be shown to you by somebody who is Self-realised?

H.H. The quality of 'real I' is to see everything in oneself and see oneself in everything. The quality of 'false I' is to regard oneself as an individual separated from everything and see everything as separate from oneself. As we proceed up the Ladder our 'false I's' fall back, and the realisation of 'real I' — the unity of 'real I' with everything — starts to grow, and we see it growing. Once it has fully grown, all of the 'false I' will have disappeared. If in our ignorance we cannot see or think of 'real I' we are led the wrong way and towards misery in our lives.

With our personal egos, and with our secretiveness, we create wrongs around us and limit ourselves: we limit ourselves and our actions. We cannot see the broad view of the universe or the Atman which is all-pervading. Because of this selfishness, and this secretive attitude of concealing our thoughts, we create barriers around ourselves.

The light of Atman is limitless and eternally shining, and it is one's own. Because it is unlimited and eternal one cannot infer that it exists separate from oneself: it is oneself. Awareness should be focussed to observe whether the Self is being experienced as Ahamkar (personal ego) or pure Aham (unqualified consciousness). To realise or to be pure Aham, all one needs to see is that the heart and mind have no more doubts or contradictions hidden or covered.

The original Shankaracharya said that those who are ignorant, and those whose knowledge of truth as Being is not firmly established, keep saying that everyone is the Absolute without real knowledge of it. Their being is still in darkness rather than light.

The possibility of evolution and increase in consciousness, even after acquisition of knowledge, is possible only in humility, with the feeling of being less than the Absolute, the limitless. Feeling proud of being all wise is an impossibility in wisdom.

The key word is Aham, which means "sense of individuality". If ego is connected with the body then it becomes Ahamkar—Kar is 'vehicle'. So if the bodily vehicle is attached to Aham then it is Ahamkar (impure ego), but if it is unattached and so united with or immersed in Paramatman then it is pure Aham.

An individual's personal ego exposes the state of his being and understanding at any moment, with his desires, ambitions and worries. True knowledge, a rational approach, justice and mercy, fellowship, etc. are its better manifestations. The purified state would manifest desires of a universal nature. When there is no limitation of the universal to the individual, there is no personal ego.

Ego always makes claims, and all claims are limited. When ego aspires to reach the limitless, it can only do so by disclaiming limitations. This is the essence of all wisdom. When all claims are dismissed then the individual is free, he does everything right, and for him there is no difference between the individual and the universal. When ego is purified, through discrimination, then the soul becomes transparent: inner and outer are no longer separated by impediments. Once this wisdom dawns then one can begin to live in freedom with or without possessions within the world: one can use them, but not as their owner.

As an example of attachment—a young man left for Bombay from his village, and four months later his wife gave birth to their son. This young man had to stay in Bombay for twelve years, for he could not afford to come home. But correspondence continued and in due course the boy could read the letters and reply to them. One day the boy wished to go and see his father so he went to the station to start his long journey. At the same time the father, now an older man, wanted to come home and reached the same station.

The father had to stay the night because the village was far away. On the same evening they were both at the station. The father got a waiting room at the station to spend the night, while the boy, having no money, had to sleep outside. The man could not sleep because the boy outside had a cold and was coughing a lot. He called the stationmaster to remove the boy from the vicinity of the waiting room. So the boy was removed and suffered much.

In the morning as the man was about to leave for the village he found some similarity in the boy's facial characteristics and enquired who he was. The boy gave his name, that of his village, and his father's name. The man asked him why he was here, and the boy said he was going to Bombay to see his father. The man realised this was his son, and embraced him and cried for the sin he had committed last night—to have removed his own son because his own son's coughing had disturbed his sleep.

When your soul is pure and love prevails, then all your promptings—whatever message you get from your conscience—will stand up for everyone in the world, not just your own son. Because Atman is the same everywhere, one sees Atman and not the son.

☆

The difference between personal ego and universal ego can be described in this way:

We have a physical body and this body usually has a shadow. In fact this shadow has no independent existence. It is produced because there is some physical source of light which by the laws of nature creates a shadow. Whatever movement the body makes will be reflected in the shadow, but the shadow has no reality in itself. It only exists when a light source shines from outside the body.

With the light of the Self—true Knowledge, Consciousness and Love—there is no shadow of anything and so no personal ego.

Conflict

There are two kinds of laws. One is called Dharma— Natural Laws or Laws of nature—and the other Neeti or man-made laws. The relation between them is like that between husband and wife. If both agree, there is peace, prosperity and contentment. But if they are in conflict, there will never be much peace in the house: just eternal conflict.

Those who understand the Laws of nature, and those who administer man-made laws are respectively like a lame man who can see but cannot move, and a blind man who can move about but cannot see in which direction he is going, or what will come out of his activities.

So a way should be found for these two kinds of people to work together: the blind man should take the lame man on his shoulder. The lame can advise the blind which way to walk and so get around and do the job. That should be the relation between men of wisdom and public men—men of the market place or government. If that relation could be maintained, the house of the nation would have peace.

But in the case of conflict nothing can be done: the blind will run the wrong way, and the lame will only talk, and the nation will in the end disintegrate.

Q. H.H. has said that a nation is purified by purifying its individuals. It seems to concern memory. Diversity in the world is part of its beauty, but at the moment the diversity is leading to conflict. How can the attitude be encouraged so that beauty, and hence diversity, is part of the plan? Some of the differences seem connected with memory, the cultural memory of the people.

H.H. Variety and diversity in creation are necessary because it is the will of the Absolute: it is for the entertainment of the Self. But when someone becomes attached to one or other aspect, hate is introduced which creates strife and conflict. It is not created by the Absolute. One should, therefore, try to refrain from such attachments.

If one is unable to eradicate attachments from the minds of others, at least one should try to eradicate them from one's own soul. When one has a strong desire to get rid of attachments and hatred, then some help can be given with love and affection. Those who remain set on strife and separation at all costs, due to hatred, cannot be helped by the scriptures and wisdom.

The simple message is that, unless one is ready to enquire, listen and act with love, one cannot be helped to transform one's unhelpful tendencies or habits. God has not created a quarrelsome universe, but a loving one. In this loving universe some take it very rigidly and get attached to only one aspect of the drama as the only reality. They cannot tolerate another view and so create conflict and do not hesitate to destroy others.

Science

Scientific work proceeds at great speed towards marvellously complex manipulation of material substances. But the inventive force of scientific knowledge leads towards complexity and expansion, and cannot by its own nature turn towards simplicity and unity. It has nothing to offer to escape from complexity. In this unrestrained march of complexity the unfortunate victims are the senses, Manas and Buddhi. They lose their sattvic lustre, and the way to liberation is almost never remembered. This is why scientifically orientated people do not retain belief or faith in the spiritual aspect of creation. Their domain of existence is either tamas or rajas.

To lift them out of this state of agitation is a tremendous job. It would require understanding of spiritual truth and its flawless practice in everyday life to attract their attention and curiosity. Only then can a turnabout take place. One thing is certain: the human mind is such that it can rise from the deepest levels of destitution, degradation, pollution or alienation. But someone has to show or become the beacon of light. In the absence of such light of wisdom and truth of the spiritual realm, it is no wonder that they have no faith and belief. Some even cherish hate and disgust towards it.

In order to help in this situation Manas and Buddhi must be purified and filled with sattva so that they can merge in the great principle of intelligence (or soul of the cosmos). Only when the intelligent and faithful tread this path of enlightenment would full experience and proper use of this principle become a practical proposition.

The realm of spiritual knowledge is the ocean of love. Love can never pressurise nor can it dictate. It is like light. If people prefer to close their eyes to it then nothing can be done. Scientists will continue to stumble in agitation until they find some peace of mind. Only then would those who have already merged in the ocean of love and wisdom be able to mount a rescue. As all things have sattvic, rajasic and tamasic qualities, so also does personal ego which, if nourished with sattvic knowledge, love and bliss, and if opportunity knocks, something could be achieved.

Scientific work is not all bad. Material substances are wonderfully used as never before. Science is very attractive and brings much comfort, but only for the physical body. It deprives Manas and Buddhi of brilliance because it simply does not deal with them. It cannot deal with them. Scientific knowledge and achievement is intoxicating, and those who are intoxicated find difficulty opening their eyes.

But it is a general rule of nature that the power enshrined in the subtle world is far greater than in the physical world. The power of water is greater than earth. Fire is more powerful than water, and air is more powerful than fire. Space, in which everything in the universe has its place, is even more powerful. The subtlest of all—the Absolute, the Consciousness—is supreme.

Q. What is it that divides the spiritual world from the world of scientists?

H.H. Scientists deal with tangible matter: their approach is empirical. They want verification of every aspect of their knowledge, which is of the physical world.

They have achieved great heights in their work and have made available much greater physical ease and comfort. But their search comes to a stage where they cannot analyse any further. Fortunately now there are some scientists who admit that there may be something beyond what they have seen and can verify but which they do not as yet know.

Soon these people will ask why it should not be known . . . and will realise that there is knowledge of another world which is beyond verifiable work on the empirical level . . . which impels, inspires and commands, orders, appreciates and creates concepts for which there is no empirical verification possible.

☆

4 *Liberation*

Q. His Holiness has said that the Realised man is steady and still in his knowledge and being, and the same in praise and blame. How does one act rightly when the need arises without judgement of good or bad?

H.H. The test of such a person is that he remains in stillness and equilibrium whatever type of duality presents itself in his worldly affairs. To be still is to enjoy the glory of the Self, which is deep, lively and full. In that experience of the great glory he needs nothing else, so that he remains totally unattached and accepts everything as it comes, whether with praise or blame. He takes no notice of fluctuations. Worldly and spiritual activity become one and the same, such that wherever he happens to be, whatever he is doing, is all spiritual in form and content. He does so because he has realised that the whole of creation is a great drama. Gain or loss, praise or blame, good or bad is part of the passing show.

☆

There is a clue in the word 'drama' which is always performed by a single company. So Rama and Ravana both belong to the same company and the director loves them equally. A good drama enacts everything as real. Rama and Ravana fight a battle and one of them is victorious. Next time the Rama actor takes the part of Ravana and gets the beating, but, having played their part, they get together as actors bearing no grudge, no hate, no pride and no shame.

The play simply feels real but remains a drama. The company belongs to the Self, and Rama and Ravana to the soul.

☆

Duality is not so much outside as inside. Sometimes we become Rama and sometimes Ravana according to the flow of our emotions, desires, ambitions and temperament. Victory does not go to Rama nor defeat to Ravana but to good and bad nature. By not allowing oneself to be overwhelmed by these parts, by retaining equilibrium, one will become stable or unshaken. With an abundance of good influences one feels peace and love, but when one is agitated and sees evil then an abundance of bad influences has taken over. Thus, the basis of duality is within, arising from ignorance. Discipline and knowledge are given to purge the duality from within. The victory is not for pride and ego but for humility and magnanimity to bring about equilibrium.

☆

Q. H.H. said, "Man never remembers himself, but if he could everything would be different for him." When I first saw you arrive at the gates of Ram Nagar I recognised that here at last is the embodiment of Self-remembering. So I watched to see, "how a Realised Man speaks and acts." (H.H. smiles in recognising his own words.)

H.H. Realisation makes it possible not to forget oneself. We are men and have been told how to live. Once we know this, it is not important to remember that we are men and should behave accordingly. But when we see men behaving like animals, then we must remember what the difference is between men and animals and correct such behaviour by lifting up our Being.

After constant meditation and work on oneself the adept starts to realise that a man is not just flesh and bones: he has a soul, he has consciousness, and he is bliss. When he has realised this fully, everything becomes simple for him. Whatever he does, the way he moves, the way he talks, reflects the dignity of Atman which is pure consciousness and bliss.

Liberation means freedom to act. People can follow the Way which suits them best as most Ways prescribe cleansing and purifying of the soul from impurities remaining from previous actions. These have to be totally removed through disciplined work. If true knowledge is properly understood after questioning, reflecting and analysing, and if meditation is practiced regularly and as simply as has been given, then one begins to progress on the Way. The more one progresses the more knowledge one gains. There is no reason why this should not be so.

Freedom & letting go

Q. H.H. seems to epitomise total freedom for the individual and mankind. Mainly this seems to be the discipline of remembering who is the provider of this freedom, found in complete stillness. How do we experience freedom?

H.H. Proper understanding of the concept of freedom is necessary. Freedom in Sanskrit is "Swatantra". "Swa" means Self and "Tantra" means discipline. Thus a free man is one who is self-disciplined. Self-discipline means that all those factors of one's physical, intellectual and emotional activities which are not useful for the Atman, must be controlled by oneself and not by anyone else. Whatever is useful and good for the Self should be accepted and put into practice. Even if pleasant things, physical, intellectual and emotional, are harmful to the Self in the long term, they must be curtailed. Discrimination and good company will help one recognise the difference.

The latent powers of the Self manifest with the growth of self-discipline. This provides confidence and clarity as one begins to act freely and naturally. The opposite of self-discipline is dependence, when one has no control of actions or discipline in oneself. When sensory pleasures, temporary gains, and a sense of power for the sake of future inheritance motivates one's actions, then one is not free but dependent. One who refrains from useless actions carried out in ignorance, and behaves naturally in the light of the Self, is free. Such actions leave no undesirable mark behind.

Internal experiences manifest in two ways. One works through the heart and the other through the intellect. The first is called the way of Love, and the second the way of Knowledge. Dr Roles worked from the heart: he did not worry too much about the way of Knowledge. Both ways lead to the same destination, which is when everything is lovingly experienced as oneSelf. Neither is superior or inferior. Both ways are true and valid.

A man who owns a small estate, on acquiring a bigger one, feels freer because he can manipulate more resources than he was used to. But this is not real freedom. Real freedom is achieved by realising that you are one with Truth, Consciousness and Bliss and so not attached or identified with anything at all. That is the true freedom. In that you merge, losing all personal identity.

If one can keep one's mind really open—open to good influences without any attachment to success or failure, without any agitation in the mind, or laziness in handling anything which comes before us in the course of our daily life—then in spite of all difficulties arising, one will keep on improving one's inner being and the world in which one lives. That is the way to live.

Discrimination & choice—Buddhi

Viveka (which means discrimination between the Real and the unreal, between the permanent and the impermanent or transient) attends exclusively to the Atman and ignores everything else. Atman is universal, constant, all pervasive, light and conscious. All that is not of Atman is limited, unstable or transitory, partial, heavy, dark and not conscious. With Viveka one sees Atman everywhere in everything at all times. A wise man, with Viveka, treats everyone as himself and sees the Self in everyone. He is always awake, just, merciful, full of love and happiness all the time. Such qualities arise from the light of Atman. Everything else arises from ahamkar, or personal ego. This assessment must come from the experiencer himself as no one can decide for anyone else, although the effect will be obvious to others.

Buddhi is like the driver of a car with Atman being the owner. When Atman wishes to go places, the driver first checks all gadgets, fills up with petrol, water and oil and gets the car ready for use. The owner (Atman) then takes his seat while the driver takes instructions from him before driving off. Having followed the instructions and arrived at the destination, the driver gets out and opens the door for the master.

If the driver is not experienced, then accidents can happen. If he is careful and has enough practice, then the master will be able to accomplish what he wishes to do. A bad driver may ignore the voice of the master and drive him to places which are harmful and can lead to disaster. One only needs clear vision and lots of practice to arrive at Realisation.

☆

Q. Is the purpose of purifying Buddhi to transform impressions and choose only those which are of service to the Atman? Is this the most crucial work in Self-realisation?

H.H. Buddhi is one of four aspects or functions of the soul, the others being Manas, Chitta and Ahamkar.

The function of Manas is to collect all sensory impressions from the outside, and project desires, concepts, etc. from the inside. If Manas is at peace and under one's control, then it takes impressions as they are: that is true impressions and necessary desires. If it is sensually passionate and agitated, then impressions are faulty and desires are unnecessary ones.

Buddhi uses the data received by Manas. A steady and trained Buddhi can analyse the right and wrong of any topic in such a way that its choice or decisions are useful to the Atman. An impure Buddhi will plead for wrong choices and wreck one's life. In the life of a disciple it is essential to tune one's Buddhi to make it clean and precise so as to distinguish what is from what is not. If tuned towards sattva it will receive and give sattva.

Chitta is the store of memory and attitude. A pure Chitta can preserve truth in the memory and provide a positive or useful universal attitude. Impure Chitta will have selfish, greedy or unjust attitudes: the memory would become unreliable and complexities would develop to create constant worries.

Ahamkar is called ego.

☆

Q. Is an example of Buddhi being tuned in the wrong direction, the strife between religious sects and the persecution of heretics, all that?

H.H. Wars in the name of religion and sectarian differences are the product of confusion in Buddhi. When not related to Atman, these things manifest in people's activities.

Q. Would you tell us the chief way to make Buddhi pure?

H.H. Love the Truth and leave the untruth. That is the cure. Pursuit of Truth cures and clears Buddhi. If one turns the other way, with pursuit of untruth, then Buddhi becomes muddled and the result is pain and suffering.

Q. Does the muddle arise from bad emotion, jealousy, anxiety, pride, worry and anger?

H.H. These are not bad in themselves. If used for selfish and worldly ends they are bad, but if used for Self-realisation, for spiritual development, they can be useful.

Attention

Realised Man attends to just what he is doing at the moment—if he walks he attends to walking; if he sits, to sitting. If there is attention to spare he can absorb fine impressions, and through attention recognise that they speak to him of Atman: "The splashing of the water is saying, 'I am THAT'; the birds are singing, 'I am THAT'."

Q. The practice of attention is essential to Self-remembering, and it is said that, "Attention is the only path the Buddhas have trod." Could His Holiness speak of attention?

H.H. Attention is the source of success, which is the same as efficiency. Only those on the Ladder have this, with the Realised Man having the greatest attention. Whatever he does is done with full attention. Ordinary people have only floating attention—one moment here, next moment there: neither here nor there. The practice of attention is essential in the life of any aspirant or disciple.

The difference between true will and ordinary will is that true will concerns the Truth, whereas ordinary will concerns itself with worldly matters. Truth in its purest form is that the individual and Absolute are the same. Attention is necessary for every type of action, worldly or spiritual. People attend naturally to what pleases them, but the pleasant is not always the same as the good. The good is that which leads to realisation that you are the Absolute. To move towards the good one needs discipline. The ladder of Knowledge and the system of Yoga are two ways which prepare and provide the way to Self-realisation.

When the capacity of attention to stay at one point is mastered, contemplation begins, which in its subtlest form of total stillness is called Samadhi. Artists, musicians, poets, writers, etc. also reach that point of unity and see all aspects of their creative work in one single point. Then their skill manifests in creative work.

Likewise, this Yoga system is similar to the Ladder of Knowledge. Here, the Good Impulse which initiates the move on the ladder begins with a will for Self-realisation. It is followed by Decision regarding the Truth about Self and non-Self: who am I, what is this world, what is my relation to the world and its creator, etc.? Only when a Decision is accomplished can the aspirant move with attention and some devotion to make systematic efforts. Through these efforts impediments fall away and Pull of the Way is established. This happens due to the increase of sattva in one's being and knowledge. This then clears the intellect so much that Insight and Abundance follow, leading to Turiya.

Gunas

Q. Will your Holiness speak of how to increase the concentration of sattva in the body?

H.H. There are two ways of increasing sattva guna. The first is the company of a saint. But of equal importance is right conduct during the day in respect of actions, feelings and thoughts. If these are in balance then sattva guna will prevail over the others. If unbalanced then the effect will be harmful both to oneself and to others and lead to unhappiness. Being balanced or "good" will lead to an increase of happiness merging into eternal happiness.

Q. I wish to saturate my Buddhi with sattva so that it would be stronger. I find that worry eats up the sattva and faith improves it.

H.H. The natural state of the Self is sattvic. All modifications in sattva are Rajas and everything opposed to sattva is tamas. One must be sure and clear that the Self is sattvic by nature, so there is no need to make it so. What we try to do is dispel the cloud and impurities which surround it, which are due to bad company, both physical and mental. With the company of good people and true knowledge the way becomes clear.

At times of reduced sattva one can always avoid bad company. A day in bad company is more harmful than a day in good company is useful.

If one has acquired influences from bad company, one can always remove them with knowledge of the Self. When one walks in the street and steps on some dirty material, one doesn't amputate the dirty feet but washes the dirt away with clean water. All bad influences are like dirt and can be washed away by true knowledge and meditation. Once sattva is predominant and you live naturally in sattva, then bad influences can no longer penetrate you. Company of good people and true knowledge stabilises faith and ensures sattva.

☆

Q. His Holiness has spoken fully of the Law of Three and described with examples the interaction of the three gunas. Would His Holiness now describe more fully the Law of Seven as it applies to realisation?

H.H. The Law of Seven is a repetitive motion unless there is escape from the circle by full realisation. Otherwise the movement repeats mechanically again and again. The Law of Seven according to the Nyana System in the quest for realisation is easy to understand and is very practical. There are seven stages or steps as on a ladder.

First stage is the Good Intention or Right Impulse. A pious desire or longing for liberation or unity arises in one who has some degree of attention as a result of his unselfish deeds and discipline in his life up to then. This is the start of an enquiry into one's own Self — a search for the Atman.

Second Stage is Decision, the coming to a decision after circumspection and reasoning that he can go further without doubt. The Way appears to be in line with his intention and conviction.

Third Stage is Effort in which thread-like attention begins. There is a lessoning of outward mental movements with entry into the knowledge of the Self. Regular practice in experience of the Unity of Self and Atman and righteous living leads the mind to go naturally inward rather than outward. Fine particles of matter have formed in the body which cause him to strive towards sattva.

Fourth Stage is Pull of the Way, when influences from the Way pull him away from the outside world of sensory impressions and pleasures which begin to lose their power. Doubts begin to cease and the real Self with right knowledge begin to appear. By this stage he has attained enough will so that there is no question of coming down the Ladder at all. The increase of sattva guna (Divine Love in this context) confirms this stage for the aspirant such that the pull of the spiritual world becomes greater than that of the sensory world. Even important activities in the material world no longer have as much pull as do endeavours in the spiritual field. Rather than leave the Way, he saves time from material activities to complete the work on the spiritual line.

Fifth Stage is Insight where the aspirant starts looking at himself and other things as they really are. He adopts right values for everything: he realises about things what they are, how they are constituted, and what their properties are. He becomes unattached or identified with his body or possessions, and ceases to consider all that is in the world as outside himself. He gets glimpses of the fact that he and the "outside world" are one and the same. There is a feeling of unity with the material world—unity of spirit with materiality.

Sixth Stage is Abundance, the stage where the outward pull is nearly gone, and he is filled with abundance of sattva or Divine Love and happiness. At this stage there is no sense of duality because Atman is seen in everything and everything in Atman. Take the example of a real elephant and an artificial one made of felt. They may look alike but with the real elephant we watch out for our safety as we might do with the artificial one if we didn't realize it was unreal. The material world of our senses is like the artificial elephant: once we recognise the distinction then we know the Real and establish a relation with it, not bothering about the artificial.

The last or Seventh Stage is called Turiya, the stage of the Realised Man when he knows himself, he knows everything, he knows how to DO, and whatever he does is just the right thing: right action, right thoughts and feelings all combined. Self has become one with Atman. All the degrees and kinds of consciousness are like colours which merge into white light.

☆

All activities of the human race are governed by sattva, rajas and tamas, these three gunas, which are everywhere in the world. When particular situations arouse dominance of one, then we feel it. When good people assemble together, one can see the rising of sattva and experience it. Whenever we go to a temple or other holy place, in the jungle or along the bank of a river, the sattva in us unites with the sattva in the atmosphere of such places and we feel united and happy. In contrast we feel starved of sattva in unsympathetic situations.

☆

The gunas relate to the Law of Three. Of the three, sattva and tamas are the two poles with rajas being the interaction between them. Time can be taken as an example. There is a past and a future with the present at the interaction between them: the future passing into the past is called the present. Such is the position of rajas or present—though it is always there, it is not dominant. Man lives either in sattva or tamas, but rajas is always there, which signifies all activity of the present moment.

Sattva is the natural state of man, while tamas is the outcome of inertia. Rajas is needed to give them a push, give them impulse to go ahead, to move towards sattva. But unfortunately many people once again come back to inertia: very few go on to the natural state of sattva.

Atman is always universal. When the light of Atman operates in its purity, the effect is to expand the individual to the universal. Whatever comes from Atman is sattvic, full of light and peace. If agitation and a sense of self-importance or rigidity follows, then it must come from the realm of rajas and tamas. Therefore, one should look at the result of the experience. If it serves the universal, it is sattvic. If it serves the individual, it is rajasic or tamasic and must arise from Ahamkar being taken personally. This is the way to verify.

Four ways

If ordinary men meet good company there is a chance of improvement. If they meet bad company there is no chance. There are those, however, who are not governed by any environment. They have a germ which is individual: they will have their own way. They may not affect others, but they will surely not be affected by others. That is the quality of people who come to a spiritual path or Way: they become the aspirants, or disciples, here, there or anywhere. The Ladder or path is for those people.

Q. Is it the inner growth of something inside them which makes them independent of public trends or opinions?

H.H. Yes. Such people have a strong quality of their essence which is quite different from the ordinary material of which essences are made. It shines and will lead them to become disciples on some Way, whatever comes within range.

☆

The Bhagavad Gita is the cream of all Indian Knowledge. It describes four Ways: the Way of Knowledge, the Way of Devotion, the Way of Yoga, and the Way of Action. Meditation is common to all these Ways. On the Way of Action or Fourth Way, one works in the world but never gets involved in it.

☆

Q. On the Fourth Way is knowledge essential?

H.H. Yes. The way of the householder is in action, and there has to be knowledge for any action. But knowledge of anything is a source of both pleasure and pain. With ordinary knowledge we identify ourselves with things or events and so experience pleasure or pain. But behind the structure of such knowledge flows the true Knowledge which does not bind one. This is Spiritual Knowledge which helps us to rise above the results of pleasure and pain and enjoy bliss whilst in the midst of actions. What we need is to harmonise our life with true Knowledge so that our actions become better and more precise while at the same time binding us no more with pleasure and pain.

☆

Understanding

There are two sides to understanding—one is Knowledge and the other is Being. Without the two coming together one could not have full understanding. When an ordinary person takes up a trade, he may know all the theory but not the practice although this is covered by the theory. Another person may be trained in the technique or practice but would not be able to explain the theory. Both of them are weak in understanding of the subject. But of the two, the man with practical ability but without the theory is preferable (to the theorist): which means that the man of Being is preferable to the man of Knowledge.

Unless this available Knowledge, which at most is good information, is put into constant and continuous use, it never becomes real, or realised Knowledge. Only when the Knowledge is realised does the individual become Realised. The work of Realisation is to clean out some bad habit (and there may be many of these). Replacement of bad by good habits is very necessary. Some people learn to speak well, but they can't really do anything, for they have not realised the Self. This ultimate Knowledge derived from practice is like seeds of knowledge out of which all dignified acts arise.

Ultimately Knowledge in action is all that matters.

5 Meditation

Meditation is designed to be practised only for a limited period so as to correct certain aspects of the internal body or soul of the individual. The only thing one has to do is to reach that state of total stillness where the mantra, meditation and meditator merge into one undifferentiated unity. This is all that is expected from meditation. Aspects of time, space and movement are of no consequence. One need not count the number of minutes one stays in the ocean of stillness. In the course of time, with practice, the necessary changes will occur as a matter of course. Sooner or later one will be able to stay longer in the stillness.

However subtle the sound of the mantra may be, it exists because of movement, and as long as there is movement there is separation. Thus, the climax of meditation is that one becomes One. There is nothing else: only one without a second.

☆

Meditation is not meant to be continued for a long time. When one comes out of meditation its stillness, extra energy and natural bliss are available. This stillness, bliss, love and the knowledge from the readings and discussions should help to stabilise one in every respect, and enable one to carry out one's work with more efficiency. It is a gradual process which should keep on improving, provided it is practised daily. Natural movements of the body can be controlled by will and mental movements by attending to the mantra. Some manage it more quickly while others may take longer. Ultimately Atman is the same for everyone.

The physical body is mostly governed by natural laws. Reasonable time is needed for sleep, dreams and waking periods. The sages with their insight into the subtle and causal levels (of the soul) have provided meditation to bring about complete balance in human life, and also to achieve total liberation from attachments, desires and ambitions which create agitation and restlessness. A few moments of stillness, union, or being oneself is enough to lead a reasonably peaceful life. When one goes to meet a Realised Man it does not matter if you have His company for a few minutes or a few hours. It is the union, the oneness of being which really matters. He is now always with you just as the Atman is always with you. Whatever happens, simply pick up the mantra and keep with it until it reaches unity with the Self.

The usual disturbances during meditation are caused by ideas, thoughts, desires, worries and expectations. As long as one of them is there stillness will elude one or be broken. In stillness one is with the Self which is full of energy. Some have no patience and prefer to use that energy instantly by inviting guests like ideas and worries to be solved. The stillness is immediately lost. Wisdom says this is not a suitable time to resolve worries, as it is a time reserved simply for meditation. These friendly guests can be entertained later.

☆

Even if the meditation seems to take a long time, it is alright to presume that it will go deeper and deeper to bear more fruit. Once the meditation becomes natural, which means that it is being done properly, then the whole system in the body will become natural, in the sense that you will never find the meditation absent at any time in your life, day or night, just as none of us can forget that we are human beings. When it becomes natural you will live on a very different plane, and all the necessary forces required to do any work will be easily available. There is nothing more valuable to be achieved.

☆

Q. Could H.H. say more about periods between meditation?

H.H. Apart from meditation Knowledge has been provided and that can be put into practice. The treasury of Knowledge will increase the more you spend it. You never lose any capital of your Knowledge. The energy derived from meditation and Knowledge can be put into practice by helping the world around you. Then the world will be happy and you will be happy too.

☆

On passing a law degree you then start practising, to gain experience. After fifteen years one has more experience than after one year. One does not have to pass Law finals again and again. Similarly with meditation—once you have learnt the theory and method of meditation you practise it. You go on practising the same thing. There is no need to change from one practice to another.

But as it goes deeper and deeper your experience will increase.

In India, in the beginning under the British Raj, there was a rule that no-one might ride in a carriage with four horses without permission of the government. Once upon a time there was a person engaged in the business of building carriages. He built one and harnessed four horses and then went around to try it out to see if it was alright. When he reached a crossing the traffic police stopped him and asked if he had permission. He said he had not, so they arrested him.

He later appeared in court and was let off on bail. He went around to various lawyers but they all said, "The rule is you can't ride in a carriage with four horses without permission, so naturally there is no escape for you."

Eventually he went to an old lawyer, who had learned the same law as others, but he had many years of practice to his credit. When the carriage builder approached him he said, "I will need to see the carriage and horses before giving you advice." The carriage and horses were brought. He inspected them and then asked for a fabulous fee. "If you pay me this fee I will be able to get you off."

In order to save his own skin the man paid the money. The lawyer said, "Appear on the fixed date with your carriage and horses." But the carriage builder objected, "I was arrested for only going out once on a trial run. If I go out in the carriage again, which will be to the court, I do not know what will happen to me!" The lawyer replied, "Don't worry. I am responsible for what happens."

So the carriage builder went to the court, the lawyer appeared and said, "My lord, you can inspect the horses, the alleged horses, and you will see there is only one horse and three mares, so he has not committed an offence."

The knowledge of law was the same as it was for the others, but it was the older lawyer's power of observation, after long practice, which made the difference.

☆

Today the age is mechanical, full of comfort and luxury, abundance of greed and pride. The ability to listen intently is weak, resolutions do not last and the attractions of the world keep people from meditating. Nonetheless, transformation is always possible in all ages. The wise make the most of it. One need not doubt the efficacy of meditation: with doubt there is no meditation.

Take the example of a house which contains various rooms. Tradesmen are met at the door while acquaintances are brought to the drawing room. Friends can come into the kitchen, and only a few intimate friends are allowed the freedom of the house. But in the compartments of our mind we find guests keep on entering uninvited, with some intimate desires, ideas and ambitions creeping in unnoticed to disturb our peace.

Therefore, it is necessary to make a resolution before meditating to keep out every type of thought. Even if some do enter do not entertain them, but pick up the mantra again. After such a resolution the body will adopt a proper posture and meditation can begin. If these conditions are accompanied by study of true knowledge, transformation is assured. Don't let guests keep on ringing the bell! They can be entertained later.

Q. Some of us now have more time to give to spiritual matters. How can one best use the time immediately after meditation?

H.H. It is natural to have finer energy after completing meditation properly. The discipline and the knowledge which has been made available will inspire the individual to use the energy and spare time wisely, because efficiency, precision and reasoning power will have improved. One should resolve to make best use of the time in dealing with the situation before one. Whatever spiritual activity suits one's inclination could be carried out alone or with others. But before starting any activity with great enthusiasm one must be quite sure that it won't become a source of regret in the end. This can only be decided by the individual.

When we go into meditation we reach a spiritual world where quietness prevails like that of a deep, undisturbed ocean. There is no movement—no waves, no currents— everything is absolutely stationary. This is the meditational world. When we look out from such a spiritual world our own being or Self is seen in everything and nothing else remains.

☆

Q. Meditation gives us a practical discipline. During the rest of the day it seems that we need help from a higher level to achieve stillness. H.H. has said that during a pause in our activity, we might "reflect the mantra". Could he give further guidance on what this means?

H.H. Life is a journey. When one travels by night from one place to another one comes across lampposts on the road. When light from one lamp ends the other shows at a distance, but there remains a patch of darkness between them. Similarly on the journey of life one needs energy, light and knowledge, but due to many engagements and activities one can forget the source of energy and feel tired.

In the stormy involvement of rajas it is necessary to keep the memory of the source of all energies which powers the universe. When you remember, the energy becomes available again. Help is readily available from that universal source to meet all occasions, and is acquired and stored through the act of being still. All one needs is to pause for a minute and remind oneself of that life-giving source of energy. The act of reminding oneself of the mantra should help to relieve tension and tiredness and make one fresh.

Q. What does one actually do during that pause? Does one just attend to coming to stillness?

H.H. It is different from the act of meditation. In this case the mantra is silently pronounced once in the mind without repeating it or doing anything else. With eyes closed, stay in that stillness for a minute or so. In that stillness the sound of the mantra will vanish slowly and total stillness will prevail.

The purpose of meditation is to bring one to the great stability: a discipline designed to produce sattva and the stability that comes with it. You then have to choose the way you wish to use it, either by loving or helping people, or in other ways pleasing to God. Whatever you do you will do it with more efficiency and goodness. Meditating solely for the sake of meditation will become void. So the sattva produced should be used for activities you take on in the worship of God or for your own spiritual advancement.

Meditation is the principal discipline. It is designed to improve the level of sattva. Once sattva has become more abundant in the individual then a light will appear within. If on the intellectual level he is not satisfied about certain ideas then he himself will be able to find the answers because of the sattva within. The best thing is to meditate properly!

6 Good company

Q. Could His Holiness please speak of Self-remembering in physical retirement, and say more about the true meaning of holy company?

H.H. There are three levels of company. One is the company of the Self, the Param-atman within; another is the company of the Realised Man; and the third is the company of the Scriptures—holy literature or whatever advice has been received from His Holiness. The first one—the company of the Self—is the holiest of all. Usually people don't find that company, they miss it, not because it is not there for it is always there. It is immanent, available to everyone, but people cannot find it. Holy literature can help them to find it, and the company of good people is necessary. And sometimes they can visit a Holy Man and sit in His company.

In the course of retirement one must keep good company. As you don't have so much to do you must improve the chance of spiritual knowledge, and the spiritual being, because one day the real physical retirement (death) will take over. If you have not prepared well for the next world you will find yourself hollow, and you will have to move around here and there without any substance. So now is the time to make use of all the company available.

The reason for not finding the company of the Self is Buddhi which, if more attached to worldly things, will keep you busy with the world and then you will have no time to look into yourself: you are not giving time to be with the Self. If Buddhi has been turned towards the spirit, then you will find that the Self is there and will communicate with you. It will help you in many ways as to how you should live your life. One thing is very sure: the Self will never give you any bad advice. It will not beguile you.

When, in course of travel or at the ashram, H.H. comes face to face with another fully realised man, the same blissful feeling occurs. There are no questions to ask, but to enjoy this blissful stream questions are raised, and it often happens that some totally new aspect comes to light. One cannot see a need, but what about the ocean of bliss? One must swim in it. After all, life is not just for searching, but it is also for bliss when there is no need to search. There can never be an end to good company. It is eternal, like wisdom, and very active too. To stop good company after reaching wisdom is an act of impure ego. Where there is this form of ego there is even more need for it. It refreshes everything.

Satsang is good company and can be described in three ways. The word is a compound of Sat and Sang. Sang means union, and Sat is an aspect of Sat-Chit-Ananda, the

Absolute. So Satsang is union with Param-atman. Sat also means study of the scriptures for the sake of the light of knowledge. Sat also means the company of a living man of wisdom who can give the knowledge of Truth through discourse and reasoning.

Good company offers good samskars (tendencies or habits) and bad company brings in bad. In good company one hears spiritual texts, analyses through reason and participates in the stream of love and devotion. Then all previous samskars of selfish pleasures, pride and prejudices begin to dissolve while new ones of purity, beauty, justice and love prevail.

Good company leads one towards universality and one begins to see the whole world as one's own family. One moves from the limited towards the unlimited, from imperfection to perfection. Everyone is full of pure and loving samskars but for some reason they are overlaid by selfish, material and divisive samskars. Once these are shed, the pure motive force of love will take over. This one cannot remove for it gives form to the universe and all in it. This is natural and ordained by the Absolute. It is an aspect of the ocean of bliss, expressed by waves of bliss, in which no one experiences separation, conflict, misery or sorrow.

☆

Q. Surrendering to the Param-atman and giving up the sense of being 'the doer' seems to be a shortcut to 'no samskar'. Could H.H. say more about this?

H.H. In creation everything is moving and every movement leaves a trace or effect. These effects are the samskars, and because of the movement they are subject to change—good or bad. New samskars arise in place of old. Some are deep and strong so last longer. They all exist in the soul.

Take the example of Valmiki who, in early life was a robber. He robbed people for himself and his family. He was also violent and his deeds caused misery and loss of life. With these samskars, one day he met some sages who were passing through a forest. They influenced his mind and he was ready to listen and act on what he heard. He was given a mantra on which to meditate. Due to his sincerity and devotion his violent samskars were dissolved and he turned towards purity, beauty and truth. He became a poet and his Sanskrit Ramayana is so beautiful and full of feeling that he was called the First Poet.

Stillness & rest

Q. His Holiness said that the meditation is only at the immobile level. This is what we have been attempting to discover. Could He say more about it?

H.H. The ultimate end of meditation is to reach total immobility, or the profound stillness, which is very deep.

No meter can measure it: it is without end. It is not necessary to remain in this state for a long period. Most of the time spent during the meditation is in preparation to lead one to this state. The stillness itself is the real experience of meditation.

☆

Q. In the West we want some knowledge, have a little love and seek some action. Is the system of meditation a fourth path to provide people who have something of everything but not enough?

H.H. Meditation is the medium to acquire a power or force which makes everything move, in the sense that you can use it to do any kind of work. For example, in the world there are many learned and knowledgeable people, but since their mind is not still, and their Being is not high, nothing really works through them. They may have the flesh of knowledge but not the heart of it.

Meditation stills the mind and in that stillness the possibility of this power being used properly arises.

☆

If you are in love and you want to bring the form of the lover into your heart, but it is always moving, where will the lover take the seat and get peace? So even for those who go on the path of Love, they have to still themselves. Without stilling the Being it will not be possible really to love anything.

☆

Q. When asked a question to which I do not know the answer, I feel as though someone else was answering through me. Is this so?

H.H. When faced with such a question, one should immediately discard all thoughts and keep complete stillness. At once an answer will come from whoever knows the answer. There are no new questions—all have been asked and answered. The area in which these answers are pooled has neither boundary nor obstacle.

☆

A market is a place of movement where people talk and buzz around. From a quiet distance one can appreciate the noise which gets louder as one gets nearer to it. When inside the market one participates in the din and the silence is apparently lost. With discipline one can hear the noise and also the silence in the middle of the market. By maintaining the stillness one does not become the market although participating in it.

Consciousness

The body does not hold consciousness, but appears in it. It is one consciousness and in this limitless sphere bodies seem to appear although they do not have independent existence in their own right. Light in a room does not exist by itself but comes in through the windows. The light is everywhere but limited objects exist in that light. Similarly the body is like a room and one presumes that consciousness exists inside the body, but in fact it is everywhere and pervading every part in and out of the body.

☆

Bliss pervades everywhere but reason shows that though conditions for bliss are in the physical world, bliss is only appreciated by the consciousness in the body. The body is only the instrument. When understanding of truth emerges then one realises that the physical is merely an expression of consciousness. Then one begins to appreciate the importance of consciousness in comparison to the inanimate physical world.

☆

A child is born, grows to youth, then manhood and old age, deterioration and death. Consciousness is always with the body and exists even after its death, being not subject to birth, growth, decay or death even though it seems to be so. A person who meditates properly begins to love the universal, and the individual body looks insignificant. He knows that all these appearances are a product of the mixture of consciousness and the inanimate in the soul.

☆

In consciousness there is nothing like small or large or any other qualification. The body together with the soul is the means of reasoning because it cannot be done otherwise. But the same can become an impediment. Having accepted it as the means of reasoning one can develop detachment. If one does not do so then it becomes a hindrance and ultimately the body will come to its end. In reality it is all full of consciousness.

The awakened state means being alive to the Eternal Laws which encompass the human race in eternity.

Music

Q. I felt such a profound relief during yesterday's music which came with mantra during the night and again this morning that I am sure it is what many people need. Often they don't want more knowledge—their heads are crammed full already—they need something to unravel the tensions in mind and body.

H.H. Music after all is an extension of the mantra system. Music has that quality to bring a new orientation of the atoms of which one is composed. The production of keertan, (religious music) can help those people who cannot reach a state of attention by their own wills. Such music has been created to help people to learn how to attend and to extend the faculty of attention still further. Use music to relieve the tensions of your people and bring them back again to the meditation, provided it is related to spiritual ideas.

Q. Great interest is shown by many in Indian culture. Some learn to play the sitar, others engage in Indian dancing. Would H.H. give his blessing for such activity?

H.H. External means are not so helpful in holding on to the state of permanent happiness as internal stability. We add certain things to our meals in small quantities so that we may relish what we eat. Yet they are not our chief food. In the same way, music and dancing prove helpful in clearing the mind of harmful tendencies.

Art

Q. The arts in the West are frequently in a bad state, either because they are hampered by old and worn out rules, or because no rules are followed at all. The first condition leads to dull art, and the second to very private art so that communication fails. How can we overcome these problems?

H.H. The same applies in the East. There is nothing wrong with the arts and their rules. The wrong is in those concerned with art for they have lost touch with real experience. Their experience and Being is shallow: they get hold of something old and re-fabricate it in their own way to seek cheap popularity or money. They produce too much from too little experience and their products are admired today but thrown away tomorrow. There is no depth which could stand the test of time.

Human society influenced by such hollow works and workers has also lost touch with appreciation, and thus you have the present situation. When a person of good Being takes to experience and expression, Art manifests and goes direct to the heart of people. Rules are not what matter most: it is Being and experience that matters. Raise the Being and Art will be created.

Consistency

Every individual or society knows the truth within because it was discovered long ago and has been made available to everyone ever since. Though the truth has always been proclaimed, it has not been put into practice. The proper way to act is to keep total unity and consistency between thought, word and deed. Thoughts, ideas, desires, aims, resolutions and ambitions should be spoken without distortion or concealment. One should speak one's mind truthfully. If the truth is spoken then others may respond and take a proper stand. If injustice is involved then one will be taken to task and the injustice removed. If the desires and concepts are just, they will be met justly.

☆

Q. There is a great desire to practise consistency, and the true knowledge given by H.H. concerning the soul has helped many to put this into practice. However, in the wider efforts for unity among other groups, this precious knowledge is simply not there. There is a big gap between the concept of unity and truth and a way to start to practise it. Is there some knowledge we can share with others who are looking for unity?

H.H. It is true that consistency is all that is required. Each individual, group, society, nation or religion knows that unity is the only way to peace and happiness. But few manage to acquire the sought after unity individually, socially or nationally because they do not open their hearts to each other. Their heart and mind is their own private property which they do not share with others. While consistency between thought, speech and action is not part of human life, conflicts will keep on visiting humanity. But injustice by deception cannot last for long. There is a proverb which says that untruth cannot be hidden for too long, like cow dung in water cannot be hidden: it will float to the surface. When untruth is seen then ordinary men, who do not seek either profit or power, will seek honest men. If they appear things will improve.

Religions are victims of their own making. They want one thing, they say another and to get their way they behave entirely against the Natural Law.

☆

7 Origin of religions

The spiritual world is concerned with only one subject:
freedom and the appreciation of unchanging truth.

Q. Seekers after truth follow different traditions in
different parts of the world. It has been said that the
essence of all these traditions lies in Sanatan Dharma
(eternal 'religion'). Will H.H. say something about this
with particular reference to Western Christian traditions?

H.H. People associate Sanatan Dharma with Hindus, but
this is not true. It is not bound by space and time, or
division of the human race at all. It is for the human race
as a whole, whereas a religion, culture or philosophy
develops from the vision of an individual and from the
talents expressed in the place where it arises.

   For instance Christianity, although basically coming
from the Jewish culture, was reinterpreted by the ideas
given by Christ. This was how the religion arose. You will
find nothing like this in Sanatan Dharma—it was not
created or evolved by human mind as it is known today.
There is no reference to any individual in Sanatan Dharma
although in India there are various ways in which its
principles have been applied. But Hinduism is not a
religion in the sense we understand Christianity. We have
a number of religions which could be equated with
Christianity but they are all supported on the basic idea

of Sanatan Dharma: likewise with Islam, Buddhism, Jainism and other religions.

☆

Human beings everywhere are the same and so have common desires and aspirations. One of the most universal of these aspirations is happiness. All religions everywhere have as their aim the achievement of happiness or bliss. The differences in religions are not to be found in their aim but in their rituals, which have different forms and characters according to the geographical place and historical time of their origin. If one looks behind these rituals one can see that the fundamental spiritual activities of man are practically the same everywhere.

Difficulties arise through the ages because rituals become bonds. One can try to break through these bonds and get to reality, though whether it would be possible for this to be done in the West, we in India do not know.

☆

There are two types of tradition—the general and the special. The first is broadly the same everywhere and consists of the pursuit of truth, happiness and peace. An example of a special tradition here is the ritual of the three castes which is unbreakable. Likewise in the West there are special traditions which have developed according to time and place. The best thing would be if we could go from these special traditions to the general, as it is there that real unity is possible. The difficulty is that these traditions are very deep-rooted. The one thing that can be done is to intensify effort towards liberation so that others may be enlightened. Only those who have peace can give peace.

☆

Q. Many people in the West are again turning towards inner discipline and learning to practise it. What are they looking for? What is it they desire? Not safety now, nor salvation, but Realisation: to become as their Maker intended them to be: to understand something of the Love of the Creator for the created. What does this desire mean in terms of a man's spiritual development, an advance, surely, from earlier days when the driving force in the pursuit of religion was fear rather than love?

H.H. The world is not divided between East and West, neither have the religions divided the world. The world is one and governed by eternal rules. Religions only preach these rules, which are so composed that they show what is right and what is wrong. Right is that which is according to the rule and wrong is that which goes against it. If there is any division, then the world is divided between the ignorant and the wise.

   The fear of damnation is for the ignorant and not the wise. The wise use discrimination and conform to the rule of their own accord and not from fear. Fear helps the ignorant, who are blind, conform to rules. These two should not be confused. The religion which shows fear of damnation also shows the way of liberation from fear and misery. The trouble is with the so-called "intellectuals" who see the rules but do not act accordingly. For such people it is only a matter of talking and writing.

☆

Q. Would it be possible to put new life into older religions?

H.H. The religions never get old. They are eternally fresh, so one can never infuse new life into an ever new thing. What really happens is that those who are responsible for conducting religions do not discharge their proper duty connected with the religion. They fail to connect the people to the religion in a proper way. It is for the wise men of today to bring out the truth of the religion and let people see it for themselves. Use discrimination and let true religion, which is lame, work together with statecraft, which is blind, and make use of both for a happy and peaceful life. As they are, separated from each other, both are facing decay and people have to face misery and unrest.

☆

When we talk about the first Shankaracharya we do not mean that this Tradition was created by him. It was only made available through him at a certain point in our history. The Tradition starts from the beginning of creation. The Knowledge does not come from men at all, whether Shankaracharya or any other leader of a religion. The Knowledge belongs to the Absolute and the Atman. Leaders only catch the ideas and expound them according to the need of the time, place and the people. They clothe the Knowledge in a fashion that suits the standard of the people living at the time where they happen to be. This is why the religions differ. Fundamentals are always the same: it is details that differ.

All the religions of the world like Christianity, Buddhism, Islam or Hinduism are not really what is meant by Dharma. They are fabrications around the Dharma. Humanity is one, so human beings can only have one Dharma, and that is the system of True Knowledge which has manifested differently in different religions. It is the desire and need of the time and place which crystallises into a single person who becomes a vehicle to express the True Knowledge in his own way.

Q. Has this Tradition ever been part of the Christian Tradition?

H.H. The fundamental principles are the same all over the world. In India there are sects who interpret the same Vedas differently. Difference of interpretation on a large scale results in the creation of different religions. One has to look into all of them to find the common thread, and also the point of departure.

A theme of Christianity has been suffering: that by suffering one can develop Being. In the Indian Tradition both suffering and pleasure are considered on one level. Just as one improves Being by facing suffering patiently, so can one improve Being by keeping a balanced head in pleasure. One should neither be broken by suffering, nor be deluded by pleasure. One should maintain equilibrium in both. The aim of suffering and pleasure is happiness and peace.

The first Shankaracharya said that pursuit of happiness or eradication of suffering cannot be the ultimate end, which can only be that which is Ultimate, never changing and peaceful. Thus, one should leave the changing suffering and pleasure, and work on Consciousness, Bliss and Knowledge because that is the Absolute.

Myths

Q. H.H. uses certain myths to illustrate His answers. In the West there is renewed interest in myth and stories as people turn away from factual knowledge to look for spiritual knowledge. Are these universal myths, such as the story of Adam and Eve, stored and released by universal memory? How does this relate to creative imagination?

H.H. Myths are common to all civilisations. In the dawn of different cultures the human spirit, wishing to pass on its knowledge to future generations, has used allegorical narratives to pass on experiences and insights. Myths are a combination of creative imagination and reason. There is an element of creative imagination involved in an artistic narrative though based on a factual foundation.

Myths are not figments of imagination. For instance, God is existent but not empirically perceptible. There is intuition of a power which cannot be indicated by pointing a finger, so inspired beings in all cultures try to build up a mythical structure so that those who have no direct intuition can grasp the idea and then open themselves to that experience. This is how myths arise, not to deceive but to explain the inexplicable.

Those who try to explain everything factually reach limitations and so turn to find traces of deeper knowledge from myths. Myths are messages of a metaphysical kind. They are allegorical and artistic expressions. Trying to look for history in them is rather fruitless. Each culture creates its own myths, but they are similar because they are all human. There is no particular body of myth deposited anywhere, but conditions giving rise to similar myths abound. Consciousness is creative and creativity is not copying.

Myths and questions are not new. Questions and answers are raised again and again in time. Each person finds it new but only because of the cloud in his experience. Myths have a message. The essence of all myths centres on the oneness of God. Some prefer the abstract approach while others prefer form and depict God in the drama of creation—the realistic approach.

The qualities associated with God are love, mercy, justice, charity, truth, happiness, rescue of the meek, punishment of evil and security and protection of the weak. They are there for us to learn and put into action.

☆

Myth helps to clear the clouds of ignorance. For example the sun is always shining and those who are not blind can always see it. If clouds come over then the sun can be hidden. When the wind blows the clouds away, the sun can again be seen. Myths are like winds that clear away the clouds of ignorance so that the truth can be seen again.

There are styles of literature in India which are developed along different lines, just as you have in the West. You have the Bible which contains parables, stories which are clothed in such a way as to contain spiritual knowledge in their fabric. The study of such stories from the scriptures is part of the process of knowledge—knowledge of the Truth: it is one of the recognised proofs of true Knowledge. Religious books such as the Bible, the Koran, or any of the Hindu scriptures, all speak of the same Truth. But interpreters of limited understanding, who have not related the subject to their own way of living, interpret it on their level, and there arises the difficulty. For us, as far as the Truth is concerned, there is no difficulty, no disparity, and no difference anywhere. There is a Sutra from the Vedas which says: "Truth is one but the wise express it in many ways." Only the rare and special people who are wise speak in their own language the same truth. Those who do not understand the truth, and yet try to interpret, put it wrongly.

☆

Prayer

Q. What is the difference between prayer and meditation? I would like to know how to pray truly and so come closer to experiencing the Self.

H.H. Prayer is for grace: spiritual, mental or physical. It creates space for grace to enter. It has sound and rhythm which attracts the mind to one pointed attention. The difference between prayer and meditation is that prayer is external and meditation is internal. Prayer is mostly aimed towards the Lord and, therefore, is external—from the Self to the deity—movement reaching out for grace. Meditation is complete withdrawal from the outside world, or ideas in the mind, and moving into the realm of oneSelf where there are no thoughts, desires, prayers or worries. It seeks nothing, not even grace. It is for union with the cause and centre of all that creation stands for—union with the Being of the Lord. It leads to the ultimate treasury, the Being, the Self, the Absolute. Prayer seeks unity while meditation is unity.

If one is afflicted by worries and agitations and cannot easily meditate, then prayer is helpful because of the sound and rhythm of the message contained in it. This will give the scattered mind some rest and so facilitate meditation. Prayer has a cause while meditation is for the causeless.

☆

Prayer must have love behind it to give it purpose and meaning. In general it should be short to be powerful. A long prayer can become stale and dry. The real seat of prayer is in the heart, and not on the lips. A prayer is not a prayer if it does not arise from the heart. All important activities should begin with prayer. Most of the Vedas are prayers.

☆

The prayer that arises spontaneously from the heart is the purest and most powerful. Written and repeated prayers are less effective unless there is enough attention to the content of the prayers, to the real meaning of the prayer. The effectiveness of traditional, repeated prayers is doubtful unless they touch the heart, although in their origin they must have been powerful. The power of the spirit lies mostly in spontaneous prayer, which may not be in beautiful words. The power of prayer is held in its meaning—the verbal repetition of a prayer is not of primary importance.

☆

Q. If one has one overriding desire which becomes a constant longing to serve only the Atman, can this be a prayer? It does not seem to need words.

H.H. A longing only to serve the Atman is certainly a potent prayer, but to continue it has to manifest in constant service, service to the whole universe which must be continuous: it does not end with a single gesture. A warm glow in the heart is the initial stage of such a prayer.

☆

Q. Could I ask about the practice of the Christian prayer, "Forgive us our trespasses as we forgive them that trespass against us."? While I see the necessity for forgiveness with my head, my heart remains cold and hostile.

H.H. The human soul is hungry for unity, and this hunger is natural and very strong. To satisfy this hunger the soul takes to prayers which are effective only with understanding. Without it they do not do much.

Prayer is not a petition to fulfil one's needs. Such a petition does not work. A real prayer from the heart simply reminds one of one's own powers which are always there but forgotten. The Creator is not mean: everything is provided for everyone. All the powers are lying dormant in our soul, and true prayer simply sheds light on that hidden power which, when recognised, becomes operative. When that hunger is satisfied one can use that power for universal goodness. The small family becomes large until "the world is my family." Once this flow of emotional energy is put into practice then God becomes a practical reality.

Knowledge from prayer reveals that so much has already been provided within but, due to personal ego, it has remained concealed. The realisation dawns that one has always tried to take and not give: one takes with a large hand and gives with a small hand! When this shell of ignorance is removed then the spirit of forgiveness, or the power to give, wakes up. In true understanding of prayer the heart must warm up with a glow, and the light of love and unity must spread.

Hunger for unity can only be satisfied by unity, which begins with association with others: the more the association the more the satisfaction. Association with the universal force, or God, means happy association with all. Prayers are not for someone out there to answer, but someone within to fulfil. One is forgiven only when one has forgiven.

If one can contemplate, meditate and reflect the deeper, inner levels of oneself, the true promptings will help one to break from the circle of birth and death through enlightenment. This urge for liberation is expressed in this threefold prayer:

Lead me from the unreal (untrue) to the real (true)
Lead me from darkness to light and
Lead me from death to immortality.

The Self is the real, the true, the light and the immortal. Those who persist, reach that state of illumination from where there is no need to fall into the coarser levels through birth. Even these prayers imply a spirit of enquiry into the knowledge that there is some truth, some light and immortality which can be realised through the grace of a teacher, the scriptures or the Atman. One who seeks will find.

☆

Oh my Lord, my whole being is Yourself, and this mind
Which has been given to me is your consort.
The life-force, breath and energy which you have given me
Are your attendants.
My body is the temple in which I worship you.
Whatever I eat or wear or do is part of the worship
Which I keep on performing at this temple.
Even when this body goes to sleep I feel
I am in union with you.
Whenever I walk, I feel I am going on pilgrimage to you.
Whatever I speak is all in praise of you.
So, whatever I do in this world in any way is all aimed at You.
In fact, there is no duality in this life of unity with Yourself.

This is the sort of situation, charged with sattva, which one has to find in oneself. Unity is not something which one is aiming at, but something which one has to experience every moment in every action, so that whatever one does is in praise or worship of the Absolute.

Grace

Q. How can one escape from the wheel of birth and death?

H.H. Creation is governed by the laws of nature which are the expression of love. Nature assists those who seek transformation and punishes those who are attached to rigidity and do not want to change.

There are three sources of help. They are a Realised Man, the scriptures, and the Self. They can be seen as teachers or grace. The company of a Realised Man is a living force and grace. His wisdom and example can free one from attachments. The scriptures are passive sources of grace. They explain the process of release and when put into practice by the aspirant the bonds of ignorance and attachments can be broken. The third and most hidden source is the Self, or Atman, which is always present, but remains unknown. If one can contemplate, meditate and reflect the inner and deeper levels of oneself, true promptings will help one to break that vicious circle through enlightenment.

But there are those who are so proud, arrogant and hypocritical that they will not turn towards the truth. They are fully satisfied with whatever they have, and due to their attachment to their possessions, they are punished by nature to keep returning again and again. The escape route is through the company of the Realised Man, the Scriptures or the Self.

☆

Here is an example of grace.

There was a handicapped man who could not move and had to depend on the charity of others. People were annoyed by him and ridiculed him for begging. Once a holy man came by and this poor man sought his advice. The holy man made sure that his advice would be fully and truthfully followed. He took the man under a tree and placed him as comfortably as possible and instructed him not to accept any charity for three consecutive days.

The villagers saw this holy man settling him under a tree. They became curious and asked the handicapped man if they could help. But he refused all help. Even when they insisted he refused, obeying the holy man from Self respect. This reliance on the Self made him strong and his face lit. Within these three days the villagers became aware of his inner force because all his worries and frustrations had totally disappeared.

This made the ultimate change and they looked after the man, and the man looked into the grace of the Self. He was provided with all that a holy man would need, and he provided all that the villagers needed to turn inward.

The company of a Realised Man is good enough to change the course of a wretched life into a holy life. The advice that "I need nothing" transformed the situation.

All doctrines and Scriptures say that Param-atman can be reached by going through some established system of discipline. But we see people who have tried them all and yet achieved nothing.

The reason is that, for the union with the pure consciousness of Param-atman, we cannot lay down any laws as Newton did for the physical universe, and then be sure that everything will go accordingly. Union with Param-atman is achieved solely by His grace, when His heart melts on seeing the rock-like determination of the devotee.

☆

Faith

Q. H.H. spoke of faith—faith on the part of the disciple in relation to the teachings of the Master. This has a strong appeal to us but our difficulty is that the word "faith" is understood in different ways. Does faith imply acting upon your belief?

H.H. Faith has two levels. The first level is that after hearing the discourses of a teacher or wise man, somebody may feel interested and attracted. But if this is not pursued, and knowledge is not gathered, this will die down sooner or later. The second level comes if the advice is taken firmly and put into action. This will then slowly deepen until it becomes full. Then there will be no doubt as to what is coming through the Teacher.

☆

Q. The word guru is sometimes used for teacher. Could H.H. explain further?

H.H. The word guru is made up of two components. The first being G and U, the latter being R and U. The first part symbolises the disciple who is engulfed in ignorance and is pressing towards the teacher. The other component symbolises the light and the teacher who is ready to bring him into light, liberty and freedom. The concept of the guru is one who takes the disciple from ignorance and brings him into the open light of Knowledge. This is possible only if the disciple's faith is established in the guru. This is essential.

Mercy

Q. He used the expression, "mercy of the guru". Is it like the mercy a judge might show to a prisoner?

H.H. There are two chief words for "mercy" in Hindi. One is used for such situations as a prisoner in court pleading for mercy. A higher form is used for example in the story of the Good Samaritan. Mercy is neither demanded nor given. It simply happens just as water flows to a lower level by its nature. When the faith of a disciple is established in the Teacher, the flow of mercy is spontaneous: it happens. It is neither shown by the Guru nor expected by the disciple.

(FCR recalled the words of Portia in Shakespeare's "The Merchant of Venice":

> *"The quality of mercy is not strain'd,*
> *It droppeth as the gentle rain from heaven*
> *Upon the place beneath: it is twice bless'd;*
> *It blesseth him that gives and him that takes.")*

Sacrifice

Q. Is sacrifice the final surrender of one's attitude to worldly attractions or does one need to practise it regularly?

H.H. Sacrifice is an important factor of spiritual discipline for realisation of the Self. Liberation means that the Self is liberated from possessions and attachments. When Self alone remains then it shines in its full glory and needs nothing else.

In moments of heightened experience, such as under the influence of scripture, a teacher or wise man, one may easily resolve to sacrifice everything. But putting that resolution into practice is difficult without proper understanding. Possessions are for pleasure, and pleasure comes from external things. Bliss (happiness) comes from within when there are no possessions.

Sacrifice leads one to that state where bliss can arise in full consciousness of oneSelf, which is the true Creator of all glorious things in this creation. By sacrifice one loses nothing but gains the Absolute. Worldly affairs carry on as the drama unfolds bit by bit, while the witness—the Self—remains in bliss. He remains in the centre where there is nothing but which is the cause of everything.

Q. Would His Holiness say more about sacrifice?

H.H. Sacrifices are of two types—external and internal. Worldly possessions, which one acquires or hoards for pleasure on demand, are the subject of external sacrifice. They come with attachment and, therefore, are an object of bondage which is a hindrance to Self-realisation. External sacrifice is a gradual process which makes one lighter—it lightens the load. Those who desire to realise the Self have to sacrifice their burdens on the way.

Internal sacrifices are equally important. Within the soul of everyone there are valued possessions of love, hate, attachments, desires, anger, greed, pride, prejudice and ego of various types. These too need to be sacrificed to unload one's mind in order to purify one's soul. These are subtle possessions which can be hard to part with. Gradually all external and internal possessions have to be sacrificed. The final sacrifice is the pride of sacrifice itself. The ultimate realisation is to 'own' nothing but the Self which cannot be sacrificed because it is limitless. What remains is Truth, Consciousness and Bliss—the non-dual Self.

Both external and internal sacrifices make one light, and with lightness one feels free. An overloaded boat sinks deeper in the water and moves very slowly. A lighter boat floats freely and moves faster to reach the destination quicker.

Devotion

It has been found sometimes that intellectuals do not respect the feelings of those more devotional whom they consider somehow inferior: not up to their standard or dignity or position. Devotional people may be more impulsive but with reasonable knowledge that impulsiveness can be channelled to become a positive, creative force. The real force lies in devotion, but knowledge is equally necessary. It is 'intellectual logicalism' which should not be encouraged as this can lead to discord.

☆

Q. We have been given much knowledge but it is the practice we are still short of. How can we make our devotional work more systematic, how to melt the heart, how to have more faith?

H.H. If the rational side of a person is more dominant you will find that they are very active with too many preoccupations with which to keep busy. But those who have more devotion, and simply resort to knowledge to help themselves, then this creates a marvellous balance and you find depth in their being.

☆

It is devotion which offers nourishment to the intelligence. If the devotional side of the human race is starved, then you will find that the world plunges into all kinds of conflicts. If you find people who are too busy, they should cut down on their 'busyness' which expends much energy. Peace is the process of consolidating energy.

☆

When we chant the word of God (Keertan) with devotion, an atmosphere is created which establishes relation with the energy of God. There are different ways of devotion: to study spiritual literature, sing spiritual songs, give physical help to others, to worship, to pray, or to meditate. But it has to be done inwardly as well as outwardly. The Vedas describe three ways to Self-realisation, or union with God: Devotion, true Knowledge or Reason, and right Action.

Action means to do everything right for the sake of God. Through Devotion the devotee keeps God in memory, prays, adores and does everything in praise of God with heart and body. When he takes his meals, he takes the food and drink as a gift from God, which in turn helps his being to be more devotional.

On the way of Knowledge questions are asked about the origin of everything. Constant searching leads to speculation about the unknown, which can lead to Realisation.

Now there is the Fourth system, of Meditation, which is designed for everybody (householder). Any and everyone can afford to buy seasonal fruits, but only a few can afford to buy out of season fruits. So it is with this meditation which is seasonal for our time.

☆

8 Compassion and forgiveness

Q. Young people are full of compassion for the sufferings of the innocent, such as children orphaned or injured by earthquake. How can one help them to accept this and see it as part of a perfect creation?

H.H. Youth is full of compassion. It does not want to see misery, but it does not have the vision of perfection, which can be disturbed by the misuse of freedom. Some misuse freedom to cause misery, whereas others use there freedom to help and create civilisation to meet disruptions with least suffering. Nothing happens without a cause, but the cause is always in the past, which one cannot get hold of to remedy the present. It is a more enlightened attitude to infer the cause and avoid its repetition in future. If someone could freeze perfection for all time, everyone's freedom would be denied.

The devastations and miseries of today are caused by the deeds of yesterday. It is not always possible to understand exact causes, but from effects one can infer the causes. The universe is perfect for one who has insight and the vision of total unity, who fears nothing but acts with great compassion whenever misery breaks out. Such a man takes steps to eradicate misery and provide alternatives to minimise the suffering if it happens for some reasons unknown.

Misery seen with wisdom can be used as an opportunity to do good and make a better world. To cry over spilt milk is an act of ignorance. With knowledge and reason, develop your inner eye and you will be able to transform misery and suffering into love, charity and a better civilisation. You might then begin to see perfection somewhere behind the remedies brought about by miseries and sufferings.

Love thy neighbour

We should cultivate the habit of never thinking of the defects of others, nor of our own. Our attitude should be to overlook and ignore them. Let good thoughts prevail. Let there be purity in our practical life.

Q. H.H. has been gently leading us to the greatest simplicity of all—total faith in, and love of the Param-atman so that we can realise that we "have nothing of our own". We need warmth of heart more than anything else so that "feel, say, do" arises from love and humility. Please can H.H. help us in our longing to act only from love?

H.H. In the Vedas it says of Brahman: "Before the beginning of time the Absolute existed alone so His desire was to create many." The entire motive force which manifests this creation of animate and inanimate variety is love or bliss. The galaxies, stars, planets, creatures and everything else are set in motion by this conscious force—love. Every bit of creation is part of the Creator, and everything is playing its part according to the conscious charge which animates it. The Leela (play) is for the pleasure and satisfaction of the Absolute, taking place with Him and within Him.

While this play is proceeding, some forget their part and the source of the motive force. The result is limitation (by superimposition). Love for one turns into hate for another. All limitations are governed by limitations of time, space and qualities (the gunas). Through ignorance these limitations become hard, binding and complex.

Only true knowledge, love and devotion can dissolve them, and in simplicity the troubles arising from complexity disappear. The universe is one and perfect within the Absolute, and it is His will that it should remain so. But in illusion and agitation everything seems incomplete, separated and alienated. The fullness, perfection and unity held in love is then shattered, and in this ignorance everything looks small. In order to escape from this, meditation and true knowledge, love and devotion are the way to unity.

These ways do not belong to any one individual, group, society or nation for all such concepts are limited and binding. They are in truth universal. Everyone in this universe is looking for love and deserves it, and must get it.

Dr. Roles was a very liberal and universal man with an open mind. His devotion towards the discipline and meditation was great. He was constantly working towards realisation of the fullness of the Self: always trying to find the way to the ocean of bliss. This spirit of enquiry, and the constant practice of this discipline, is needed by everyone.

The Absolute is the embodiment of love, knowledge and devotion. It is limitless in every sense and its door is always open. The universe is one and full of love and everything is motivated by love. Let love flow without hindrance from any direction.

Q. In examining myself I cannot find that I have one drop of true undemanding love. Will I have to go to the end of the Way of Knowledge to find it?

H.H. Knowledge of love is not essential for the lover because the moment one gets this knowledge that one truly loves, self-righteous pride arises and drains out what is there and can lead you away. It is good not to know what one's qualities are! Let them be there, acting through you, and do not analyse them. They are there and are plentiful, because the whole treasure of knowledge and love belong to Atman. No one is devoid of them.

Those who get certificates become subject to loss of true knowledge and love. Those who don't have certificates, but continue with devotion and effort, really find them. There are no honours or decorations on the spiritual path.

Q. At times I have had a great desire to help someone in difficulty but realise that 'I' cannot help directly, but can meditate from this desire in the hope that the right help will be given from elsewhere. Can help come in this way?

H.H. Yes, it is quite possible that help can be given to individuals if someone with a pure heart, and with a sincere desire, wanted to help them by meditating with a predisposed desire. A better way of helping others is not to have any desire as such, but to meditate so purely that there is a wealth of goodness in you to which anyone who needs help would come and take naturally. The sun does not give light to any particular person but by its presence it gives abundance of light to everyone who wishes to benefit from it. So the better way is to have more refinement or love in oneself which can be used by anyone who needs it.

☆

Q. The cry is always for more sattva. People know that with more sattva things would become right. What can we do so that there is abundance of sattva in our being?

H.H. The collection of certain good qualities is essential. These are:

1. One should always love to speak the truth so that there is no disparity between what one thinks, what one says and what one does.

2. Cultivate the love of people, encouraging them in turn to express their love through certain types of activity.

3. Be magnanimous in dealing with those around you.

☆

Dedication to the service of Param-atman and to other people in thoughts and actions at all times and in all circumstances is the way to stabilise your mind in your own great Self.

Justice & equity

Q. Your Holiness has taught us that consciousness is all around us and in us. It does not have to be created. Through this understanding a taste of what harmony really is comes with a realisation that there is an omnipotent justice in all that is manifest around us. Is the ultimate result of manifestation to bring harmony and unity, and how can we feel more justice and equity in our own lives?

H.H. Justice and equity are two sides of the same coin. It is not possible for either of them to exist alone. But they are denied by their opposite which is attachment and prejudice, which is responsible for creating difficulties in personal lives, and in social and national life. If there is any attachment anywhere there is bound to be prejudice as well. Attachment is always to a particular form, which has limitations, so there will be prejudice against anything outside those limits. Justice will therefore be denied.

The antidote is to treat everyone in the world as you would like to be treated yourself. Everyone else is the same aspect of the Absolute as yourself. You will then know what is natural equity and how justice descends on this earth.

☆

Humility

The possibility of evolution and rise of consciousness, even after acquisition of knowledge, is possible only in humility, with the feeling of being less than the Absolute, the limitless. On the other hand, if one presumes to have reached the zenith, there is no more scope for evolution since all knowledge has been acquired and full realisation has been achieved. This would be an example of going from one darkness to another. There can be no pride and no declaration of omniscience, but if there are questions one can be helped. Feeling proud of being all wise is incompatible with wisdom.

☆

Q. Is it the melting of the heart that clears out the rubbish to make room for important ideas?

H.H. Your observation is right. With good company and with good reason and discourse we allow the heart to melt so that this rubbish is cleared. Melting of the heart simply means the dissolving of impurities. Thus, the good influences will crystallise in the heart and stay there.

Q. To enable this to happen one needs a certain humility, which some pride in one prevents. Although the mind knows what is necessary, I find it cannot be done by oneself.

H.H. Yes, humility is essential for this melting of the heart. With predominantly emotional types it is fairly easy to melt the heart, which in effect is bringing the heart to its natural state. Nothing really happens because personal ego has no reality: it is only an idea which exists. Once the good ideas from good company take their place, whatever we think of as personal ego is lost automatically and illusion is gone—the illusion of a personal ego.

To bring the intellectual to the emotional state where his heart can melt, you have to answer his questions and tackle them thoroughly and well so that no more remain. As long as questions remain the heart may not melt.

It is a well established tradition in recognising the levels of Being that, as a person rises on the steps, he fails to recognise them. A person thinks of himself as ordinary, devoid of any understanding or greatness, because in merging with the outer world—whatever it may be for that person—he experiences the weakness of others as his own, and in doing so becomes humble. Humility is essential in making progress on the spiritual way.

Wisdom

Love the truth and leave the untruth is the chief way to purify discrimination.

Through the Ahamkar (personal ego) the individual exposes the state of his being and understanding at that moment, with his desires, ambitions and worries.

Without some limitation of the universal there would be no Ahamkar.

The purified state would manifest desires of a universal nature. True knowledge, a rational approach, justice and mercy, fellowship, etc. are its better manifestations. Personal ego always makes claims, and all claims are limited. When pure ego aspires to reach the limitless, it can only do so by disclaiming limitations. This is the essence of all wisdom. When all claims are dismissed then the individual is free: he does everything right, and for him there is no difference between the individual and the universal. His soul becomes transparent and inner and outer are not separated by any impediments.

☆

A holy man came and said, "I have gone through all the scriptures and now feel that I have learnt them well. Could there be some form of recognition or a certificate to that effect?" He was told that in the absence of any equipment to measure the quality and quantity of wisdom it is impossible to do so. But if there is no doubt in your mind about anything then you can presume yourself to be wise, although it will become obvious whenever the so-called wisdom is expressed in words or actions. When true knowledge becomes your own then it can be called wisdom.

☆

Preparing for death

During retirement one must continue to keep good company. Because you have less to do you must improve your spiritual knowledge and being, because one day the real physical retirement (death) will take over. If you have not prepared well for the next world, you will find yourself hollow: you will move around here and there without any grounding. So now is the time to make use of all the good company available.

Q. I am finding it easier to make efforts in a peaceful old age than in a turbulent youth. But old age means the certain approach of death. What attitude should be formed about this?

H.H. The day one comes into this world one's departure is also ordained. It is certain that one who is born must go sooner or later. But it is only the body which is born and then dissolved: the dweller neither comes from anywhere nor goes anywhere. So the only preparation is to establish complete detachment from the body. When the mortal body dissolves back into the physical elements, the soul remains until the next time round. It will only be dissolved at full liberation.

Therefore, in truth, not much importance need be given to the death of the physical body: all efforts should be aimed at preparing for total liberation. To achieve that one has to be alert and awake so that the soul can be purified through knowledge and meditation.

When all impediments are removed and no limitations remain, the so-called consciousness of the individual will merge in universal consciousness. This is the only opportunity worth looking for, and making efforts for, and should not be missed.

Two distinct directions of work have been given to help: the meditation and the knowledge. Both are valid. Devotion itself is a valid way. They both lead to liberation, or full realisation, singly or together. It is possible to realise the ultimate unity here and now by either way. It doesn't really matter if the body goes today or in ten years' time. Even when the body is incapable of engaging in physical efforts, the soul is still capable of going either for liberation or bondage.

☆

Liberation is possible when meditation becomes natural and all hindrances are removed. Through the knowledge one realises the identity of the Self as none other than the Absolute, and thus loses all concept of limitation. There is no other special way. Meditation and knowledge become special when one decides to treat them sincerely without missing any opportunity for constant awareness. On the whole the way of meditation is easier compared to the way of knowledge. Just use the will you were originally given.

☆

In real meditation there are no impediments—no influence of our thinking process, no desire and no personal ego. The ultimate effect of meditation is the elixir of life by which the individual transcends mortality, which means total liberation.

Transcending mortality is spiritual—it has nothing to do with the physical body, which has been given to us so that we may acquire this freedom.

Q. How should one prepare oneself for death?

H.H. Death is only a change of form if one is not liberated. One should follow the discipline as much as possible and withdraw from the world to devote one's mind to remembering the Absolute and dwell on the glories of His creation. The fewer the desires the better. The only need is to remember the Absolute you have known. Don't be attached to the world. The journey will be easy.

The physical body is like a garment. It is useful for a limited time. When it is worn out it is discarded and changed for a new one, only because impediments have not yet been fully cleaned from the soul.

His Holiness sends a special message to Dr. Roles that he should not retire before H.H. himself retires! Retirement is only on the physical level, but as far as spiritual work is concerned, up to the last breath good company must continue. So there is no retiring time for this Work. His Holiness blesses Dr. Roles that he should keep going and keep doing the job!

Further publications available from The Study Society

Fresh Mornings of life *An introduction to meditation*

Good Company *An anthology of sayings, stories and answers to questions by His Holiness Shantanand Saraswati ISBN 0-9547939-0-0*

The Man Who Wanted to Meet God *A collection of myths and stories, taken from audiences with His Holiness Shantanand Saraswati, that explain the inexplicable ISBN 0-9547939-1-9*

Voyage of Discovery *Sayings and teachings of Francis C Roles (New York) ISBN 0-9547939-4-3*

Prayer *A compilation of sayings of His Holiness Shantanand Saraswati on prayer*

Birth and Death *A similar compilation of sayings of His Holiness ISBN 0-9547939-5-1*

The Orange Book *A Method of Self Realisation ISBN 0-9547939-3-5*

A Lasting Freedom *Text of two lectures given by Dr Francis C Roles in New York –* Glimpses of Truth *and* Know Yourself

Who am I? What is my Soul? *Material from audiences with His Holiness Shantanand Saraswati which suggest answers to these questions ISBN 0-9547939-2-7*

The Bridge No 12 *A tribute to the life and work of P D Ouspensky by members of the Study Society*

The Bridge No 14 *A tribute to the life and work of Dr Francis C Roles by members of the Study Society*

Being, the Teaching of Advaita *A basic introduction, by Philip Jacobs ISBN 0-9547939-6-X*